Elite Warriors

ARMY RANGERS

JULIA GARSTECKI

BLACK RABBIT BOOKS

Bolt is published by Black Rabbit Books
P.O. Box 3263, Mankato, Minnesota, 56002.
www.blackrabbitbooks.com
Copyright © 2019 Black Rabbit Books

Marysa Storm, editor; Grant Gould &
Michael Sellner, designers; Omay Ayres,
photo researcher

Library of Congress Cataloging-in-Publication Data
Names: Garstecki, Julia, author.
Title: Army Rangers / by Julia Garstecki.
Description: Mankato, Minnesota : Black Rabbit Books, [2019] | Series:
Bolt. Elite warriors | Includes bibliographical references and index. |
Identifiers: LCCN 2017025359 (print) | LCCN 2017026164 (ebook) |
ISBN 9781680725421 (ebook) | ISBN 9781680724264 (library binding) |
ISBN 9781680727203 (paperback)
Subjects: LCSH: United States. Army. Ranger Regiment, 75th–Juvenile
literature. | United States. Army–Commando troops–Juvenile literature.
Classification: LCC UA34.R36 (ebook) | LCC UA34.R36 G37 2019 (print) |
DDC 356/.1670973–dc23
LC record available at https://lccn.loc.gov/2017025359

Printed in China. 3/18

Image Credits

Alamy: devilmaya, 19 (compass); Oleg Za-
bielin, 18–19 (soldier); RGB Ventures/SuperStock,
7 (bttm); airforcemedicine.af.mil: US Air Force/Airman
1st Class James Richardson, 1, 14–15 (bkgd); army.mil: US
Army Photo, 7 (top), 21 (bttm), 22 (both); US Army Photo/Patrick
A. Albright, 25 (bttm); US Army Photo/Spc. Steven Hitchcock, 8–9;
commons.wikimedia.org/acc.af.mil: US Air Force Photo/Staff Sgt. Jeremy
T. Lock, 4–5; en.wikipedia.org: PEO Soldier, 16 (machine gun); Ldopa,
18–19 (radio); benning.army.mil/defense.gov: US Army Photo, 26–27;
defense.gov: US Army Photo, 21 (middle), 24, 25 (top), US Army Photo/
Sgt. Paul Sale, 21 (top); natioanlguard.mil: US Army Photo/Sgt. Sean
Mathis, Cover; Shutterstock: Africa Studio, 31; Getmilitaryphotos, 10, 11,
16 (top); Militarist, 16 (rifle); NEstudio, 3, 13, 28, 32; santoelia, 19
(explosives); Sergei Gontsarov, 16 (pistol); Tony El-Azzi, 16 (knife)
Every effort has been made to contact copyright holders for
material reproduced in this book. Any omissions will be
rectified in subsequent printings if notice is given
to the publisher.

CONTENTS

CHAPTER 1

In

U.S. planes fly above the country of Afghanistan. One of them carries about 200 Army Rangers. An enemy landing strip lies below. Planes bomb the ground. The explosions cause enemies to run away. Now, it is the Rangers' turn. The soldiers jump from the plane. They disappear into the clouds.

Mission Accomplished

The moment they land, Rangers get to work. The soldiers search for any remaining enemies. They **secure** the strip. Then, just as quickly as they arrived, the Rangers leave. Their job is done.

Rangers take over landing strips. Pilots then use the strips to land U.S. aircraft.

Rangers can be anywhere in the world in 18 hours or less.

Who Are the Army Rangers?

Rangers belong to the U.S. Army's 75th Ranger **Regiment**. They are highly trained soldiers. They're ready for **missions** at a moment's notice. They perform quick attacks behind enemy lines. Surprise is one of their best weapons.

In 1945, Rangers saved more than 500 POWs on one mission.

CHAPTER 2

Many Jobs, MANY PLACES

Rangers go on all kinds of missions. These soldiers fight **terrorists**. They take over enemy buildings. Rangers also rescue **hostages**. They save prisoners of war (POWs).

Studying and Scouting

Rangers also go on spy missions. They sneak into enemy territories. There, they gather information and study the enemy. They record the number of soldiers. They find out what weapons they use. This info helps plan other missions.

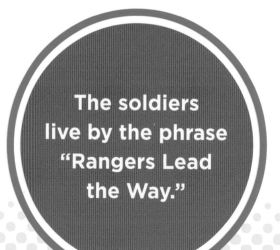

The soldiers live by the phrase "Rangers Lead the Way."

WHERE RANGERS HAVE WORKED

Rangers have gone on missions around the world. Here are a few of the places they've worked.

Grenada
1983
rescued Americans

Panama
1989
took over airfields

Iran
1980
rescued hostages

Afghanistan
2001
took over landing strip
2017
raided enemy compound

Vietnam
1969–1972
fought in the
Vietnam War

Philippines
1945
rescued POWs

Weapons Used by Army Rangers

rifle   machine gun   pistol   knife

CHAPTER 3

WEAPONS

and Gear

Rangers need weapons to do their

jobs. They carry rifles and pistols.

Rangers go on many missions at night.

Night-vision goggles help them see.

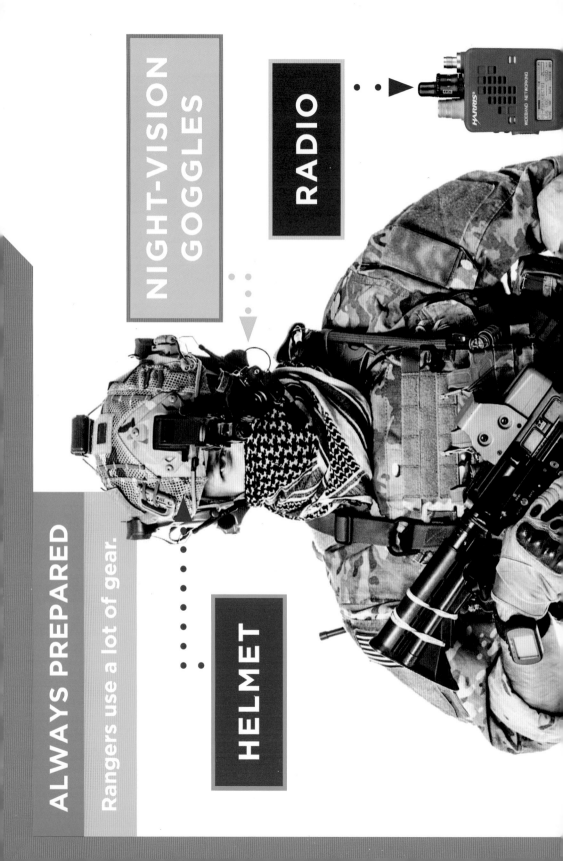

ALWAYS PREPARED

Rangers use a lot of gear.

NIGHT-VISION GOGGLES

RADIO

HELMET

EXPLOSIVES

COMPASS

CHAPTER 4

TOUGH Training

Becoming a Ranger isn't easy. Soldiers must pass the Ranger Assessment and Selection Program (RASP). During RASP, soldiers learn what it takes to be a Ranger. If they pass, soldiers join the 75th Ranger Regiment. But few soldiers make it through RASP.

Where RASP Is Held

Fort Benning, Georgia

Ranger Assessment and Selection Program

RASP lasts eight weeks. It pushes soldiers to their limits. They carry heavy gear on long marches. They train with little sleep. Soldiers learn to work as teams. They also learn how to **adapt** to their situations. Rangers must be ready for anything.

In 2016, the first female soldier passed RASP. For years, women weren't even allowed to try.

RASP

BY THE NUMBERS

12 MILES
(19 kilometers)

distance soldiers must march in 3 hours or less with a 35-pound (16-kilogram) rucksack

NUMBER OF CHIN-UPS SOLDIERS MUST PERFORM

6

8 WEEKS
LENGTH

40 MINUTES OR LESS
TIME IN WHICH SOLDIERS MUST RUN 5 MILES (8 KM)

Ranger School

Soldiers also complete Ranger School. It's some of the U.S. military's toughest training. Soldiers train in all kinds of environments. They practice fighting on mountains. They train in swamps. Soldiers who pass get the Ranger **patch**.

Soldiers Who
Complete Army
Ranger School

about
40%

Ready for Anything

Rangers are elite warriors. They have served the United States for many years. And they will protect the country for years to come. Rangers are always ready to lead the way.

adapt (uh-DAPT)—to change something so it works better or is better suited for a purpose

hostage (HAHS-tij)—a person captured by someone else

mission (MISH-uhn)—a job assigned to a soldier

patch (PACH)—a piece of cloth with an identifying mark that is sewed onto clothing

pistol (PIS-tl)—a small gun whose chamber is part of the barrel

regiment (REJ-uh-muhnt)—a military unit that is made of several battalions

rifle (RI-ful)—a shoulder weapon with grooves in the barrel

rucksack (RUHK-sak)—a bag strapped on the back and used for carrying supplies

secure (suh-KEYR)—to make something safe by guarding or protecting it

terrorist (TER-ur-ist)—a person who uses violent acts to frighten people in order to achieve a goal

BOOKS

Bozzo, Linda. *Army Rangers.* Serving in the Military. Mankato, MN: Amicus High Interest, an imprint of Amicus, 2015.

Slater, Lee. *Army Rangers.* Special Ops. Minneapolis: Checkerboard Library, an imprint of Abdo Publishing, 2016.

Stilwell, Alexander. *Army Rangers.* Military Jobs. New York: Cavendish Square Publishing, 2015.

WEBSITES

75th Ranger Regiment
www.goarmy.com/ranger.html

Ranger School – Student Information
www.benning.army.mil/infantry/ARTB/StudentInformation/

United States Army Rangers
www.army.mil/ranger/

INDEX